UNITED METHODIST ALTARS

W9-CAR-837

UNITED METHODIST ALTARS

A Guide for the Local Church

HOYT L. HICKMAN

Abingdon Press
Nashville

UNITED METHODIST ALTARS
A GUIDE FOR THE LOCAL CHURCH

Copyright © 1984 by Abingdon Press

Third Printing 1985

All rights reserved.
No part of this book may be reproduced in any manner
whatsoever without written permission of the publisher
except brief quotations embodied in critical articles or
reviews. For information address Abingdon Press,
Nashville, Tennessee.

Library of Congress Cataloging in Publication Data

HOYT L. HICKMAN (Hoyt Leon), 1927–
  United Methodist altars.
  Bibliography: p.
  Includes index.
  1. United Methodist Church (U.S.)—Liturgy—
Handbooks, manuals, etc. 2. Methodist
Church—Liturgy—Handbooks, manuals, etc.
3. Altar guilds—Handbooks manuals, etc.
I. Title.
BX8382.2.Z5H53   1984   264'.076   83-21554

ISBN 0-687-42985-4

Scripture quotations unless otherwise noted are from the Revised Standard
Version of the Bible, copyrighted 1946, 1952, 1971, © 1973, by the Division
of Christian Education of the National Council of the Churches of Christ in
the U.S.A., and used by permission.

Symbol drawings by William Duncan from *Symbols of the Church* edited by
Carroll E. Whittemore. Copyright © 1959 by Carroll E. Whittemore. Used
by permission of the publisher, Abingdon Press.

MANUFACTURED BY THE PARTHENON PRESS AT
NASHVILLE, TENNESSEE, UNITED STATES OF AMERICA

[CONTENTS]

[PREFACE]

This book has been written in response to an urgent need, expressed by a great many persons, for a United Methodist Altar Guild manual.

For many years the book that met this need in the former Methodist Church was *Methodist Altars* by Dessie Ash Arnett, Betty Isaac Stewart, and Lenace Robinette Clark. It first appeared in 1951 and went through several editions and finally appeared in 1970 as *United Methodist Altars*, just after the union that produced The United Methodist Church. This book has long been out of print, and there has been a demand in our denomination for a new manual to take its place.

In the meantime United Methodists, along with members of other Christian denominations, have experienced an extraordinary reform and renewal of their worship patterns and practices. These reforms have sought to make worship both more authentic to the oldest Christian traditions and appropriate to contemporary life, and they have been accompanied by many signs of new vitality. On the other hand, there have been many passing fashions in worship and many people who look for stability and continuity in their worship have understandably reacted against them.

In these years many United Methodist Altar Guild members have turned to recently published books in other denominations that are readily available and that take into account these recent developments in worship. *The Altar Guild* by S. Anita Stauffer (Lutheran) and *The Altar Guild Book* by Barbara Gent and Betty Sturges (Episcopal) are outstanding examples. On the other hand, the traditions and practices of these denominations are so different from those of United Methodists that their books, though they are excellent, do not meet the needs of Altar Guilds in our denomination.

The new *United Methodist Altars* attempts to build upon the strengths of the old *(United) Methodist Altars* and of the manuals of other denominations, while providing the help needed by today's United Methodist Altar Guilds.

The author acknowledges with gratitude the helpful criticisms and suggestions received from liturgical scholars James F. and Susan White and from these persons active in local United Methodist Altar Guilds: Rachel Drumright (Belmont, Nashville), Jack Inman (Belle Meade, Nashville), and Elizabeth Jones (First Centenary, Chattanooga).

Further criticisms and suggestions are invited from readers and will be taken into account in any future revisions of this book.

Hoyt L. Hickman
July 1, 1983

[THE ALTAR GUILD]

You may not call your committee or group an Altar Guild. In your church you may be the worship commission or the chancel committee. Or you personally may be the Communion steward, or you may change the candles and the altar cloths, take care of the flowers, make banners, or keep things the way they should be in the sanctuary. You may be the pastor or the custodian doing some of these things. But if you or your group have been entrusted with any part of the care of the sanctuary and its furnishings or the things that pertain to the worship services, you have a special responsibility and a privilege of the highest order. It is for you that this book is written.

How many people or how much organization you need depends on the size and character of your congregation and the sanctuary where you worship. Whether or not you have an organized Altar Guild, you should be aware of certain basic principles that apply.

1. The purpose of your service is to provide the best possible environment for your congregation's worship of God. No detail of that environment is too insignificant to matter when preparing for the

worship of the people of God. The fact that you have been given your responsibilities is a testimony to the trust the pastor and congregation place in your dependability and devotion.

2. Because the pastor is in charge of congregational worship, you will work closely under his or her direction. It is most important that you meet regularly with your pastor to study worship, share ideas and feelings, and keep communication open between you.

3. It is essential that you know your assigned duties, which may vary from one local church to another. Clarify these with your pastor and then list them on a sheet or in a leaflet. When they have been approved by the pastor, Worship Commission, or Council on Ministries, they can be used when training new persons.

4. You need a good working relationship with the custodian. You will neither direct nor replace the custodian but each of you should have an understanding and respect for each other's work.

5. You or your group are related to the Worship Work Area. If your church has organized the Worship Work Area into a commission, the Altar Guild should be represented on it (by your chairperson if you have one) and should relate to the Council on Ministries or Administrative Council through it. Materials or supplies needed can be provided from the church budget through the Worship Work Area.

6. If you have an organized Altar Guild, it should include the Communion stewards, the person or persons in charge of flower arrangement, and probably a musical leader who can help you relate to

the singers and instrumentalists who also serve God in the chancel.

7. Divide the responsibilities where possible, but do not make an Altar Guild so large it is unwieldy. Persons can take turns serving a month or a quarter at a time. If a particular responsibility such as Communion or flower arranging is too much for one individual, it can be entrusted to a committee with a chairperson. On the other hand, it is better to have fewer people performing their duties well than to have an organization so large that it cannot effectively train or use those who serve on it.

8. Give reverent care to the things that have been set apart and consecrated to sacred uses, as a way of practicing reverence for all God's creation. Yours is a very special service to God, an act of worship in itself, through which God can change your life and the lives of other people.

9. On the other hand, do not treat these things as ends in themselves so that you come to worship your beautiful church and its furnishings rather than God and value them above the people who can make use of them.

10. Men as well as women can serve in any of these capacities. Look for youth as well as adults who have abilities and who, under proper guidance, can be trained to serve. Use your imagination as you search for persons with backgrounds, talents, or skills to contribute special services.

11. Find ways to recognize and express appreciation to those who serve, especially those whose service is behind the scenes and often unknown to the congregation. At the very least, each year recognize and install persons as part of your congregational worship.

[SPACE AND FURNISHINGS]

The environment—the space—in which your congregation worships is extremely important for what happens as you worship. It has more effect on the worshiper, for better or for worse, than we usually realize. Unless worship is held outdoors, it is held in some kind of room. There is no one universally accepted name for the room in which Christian congregations worship. This room is often called the sanctuary, although traditionally the term sanctuary has been used to refer only to the immediate area around the altar table. Many people prefer to refer to the whole room as the sanctuary because God is present in, and sanctifies, the whole worshiping congregation and because the whole room has been carefully designed to help the worshiper be more aware of the sanctity of God and of God's creation.

Sometime soon, take a careful look around the room where your local congregation worships. Notice all the things that have been done in design and decoration to make that room conducive to worship. Notice any assumptions that seem to have been made as to what should happen when people worship. Notice, too, anything about the room that seems to detract from worship.

In most churches, particularly medium-sized and larger ones, there is between the outer door of the building and the inner door of the place of worship a hallway, or vestibule, or lobby, which is traditionally called the narthex. It helps us make the transition between the place of worship and the everyday world. It is a space where the bonds of Christian community are formed and renewed, as ushers or greeters or minister welcome persons and as people greet and talk with one another. On cold days it provides a place to catch one's breath after coming in out of the cold, it provides space for removing and hanging up wraps, and it protects worshipers from a draft of cold air every time the doors are opened. Everything in the room should help make it a warm and friendly space that serves these purposes. Even in churches without a narthex you can often tell when you step directly into the worship room that there is a space immediately inside the door which serves these purposes and is not quite like the rest of the room.

While rooms designed for worship differ widely in many ways, they are usually designed to draw one's attention to a focal area, usually on a raised level, commonly called the chancel, which may either be recessed behind an arch or project out into the area where the congregation sits, which is called the nave. Sometimes the room is shaped like a cross, with seating areas called transepts on either side, as in the diagram on the next page.

You will often see reference to the chancel end of the room as "east," the rear of the nave as "west," the left side as "north," and the right side as "south." This does not refer to actual geographical directions but is a usage based on the tradition that churches were built facing east, the direction of the rising sun, a sign of resurrection.

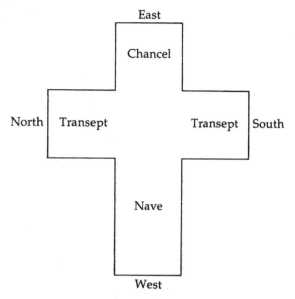

Since the chancel is where the work of the Altar Guild is centered, we should look at it in more detail. The chancel customarily contains several key furnishings.

1. A table—variously known as the Lord's table, holy table, Communion table, altar table, or altar—functions primarily as the place where the feast of the Lord's Supper or Holy Communion is held. As such, it symbolizes God's presence in the church and is the symbolic center of the church's life. It is the center of actions in our worship, uniting us to God and to one another. Every other function of the Lord's table is secondary. It is never merely a convenient surface on

which to place books, empty offering plates, and flower vases.

2. A pulpit is a stand behind or in which the minister stands to preach and perhaps to conduct other parts of the service. It symbolizes the authority of the Scriptures, which are "opened" to the people by reading and preaching. For this reason it is appropriate that an open Bible be on the pulpit and that the Scriptures be read as well as preached from there. Sometimes there is also a lectern, a smaller stand which may be used for reading and for conducting certain other parts of the service.

3. A baptismal font, which contains water, is used for baptisms. While in some denominations the font is placed at the entrance to the nave, symbolizing baptism as entrance into the church, in United Methodist churches generally it is placed in the chancel area where the welcoming congregation can gather around it and where it is in close relationship to pulpit and table. Occasionally United Methodist churches have baptistries where persons may be baptized by immersion.

Sometimes the chancel area also contains seats for the choir or choirs and an organ or piano. Also, there is usually a rail around, or within, the chancel where persons can kneel for prayer, commitment to Christ, or Holy Communion. This rail can be called the Communion rail or the altar rail. These furnishings support our sense that we are a people gathered around the table of the Lord.

There are many ways of arranging these basic furnishings, but most United Methodist churches tend to follow one of several basic patterns:

1. One pattern, sometimes called pulpit-centered, was dominant in the nineteenth and early twentieth centuries and is still fairly common. There is a raised platform with the pulpit in the center, from which the minister leads and preaches. There is no lectern. The Communion table is probably in front of the pulpit, on a lower level. The baptismal font can be in various locations, but attention is not usually called to it unless there is a baptism.

2. A second pattern, sometimes called divided chancel, was dominant during the middle of the twentieth century and is still very common. In the center against the wall is a table or altar that is intended to be the center of worship. The pulpit is on one side of the chancel, and a lectern or baptismal font is usually on the other side.

In recent years many churches with divided chancels and immovable altars have put a free-standing Lord's table well in front of the altar where there is room to walk around it. Such a table can function far more effectively as the Lord's table than can the altar against the wall.

3. In the last generation a variety of arrangements have been tried, with none clearly dominant to date. Most of these patterns, however, center around a free-standing Lord's table in the middle of an open space, with pulpit usually to one side and sometimes balanced by the baptismal font on the other side.

No matter what the arrangement of space and furnishings in your sanctuary, the work of the Altar Guild (or its equivalent in your church) is centered in the altar table and its immediate surroundings. So we need to look more closely at the table itself.

Photo by Bracey Holt

Tulip Street United Methodist Church, Nashville, Tennessee, is pulpit-centered

Photo by Bracey Holt

Blakemore United Methodist Church, Nashville, Tennessee, has a divided chancel to which a free-standing Lord's table has been added

Photo by Les Turnau

Central United Methodist Church, Charles City, Iowa, has a contemporary arrangement

Sometimes the Lord's table looks like a dining table—made of wood, with a tabletop and supported by legs that can be seen. This is appropriate, since its primary function is to be the place at which the holy meal that we call the Lord's Supper or Holy Communion is celebrated and served. In the early Church the Lord's table was a real table. This has been the case throughout most of our denominational history as United Methodists. It is again the prevailing practice today.

Often, however, the altar table is designed to look more like an altar of sacrifice. It may have a solid front and be placed up against the far ("east") wall of the chancel so that the minister stands in front of it with his or her back to the congregation as though offering a sacrifice. It may be partially or entirely made of stone rather than wood. It may have a tablelike step or shelf, called a retable or gradine, rising above it at the back next to the wall, on which cross, candles, and flowers often have been placed. Above and in back of these may be a large carved stone or wood panel known as a reredos, or a hanging fabric known as a dossal.

Christians have often disagreed as to whether or not the Lord's table is properly called an altar. On the one hand, we can make no sacrifice that adds to Christ's "full, perfect, and sufficient sacrifice for the sins of the whole world." On the other hand, Paul appeals to us: "Present your bodies as a living sacrifice, holy and acceptable to God, which is your spiritual worship" (Rom. 12:1). As we remember the sacrifice Christ made for us, we pray God "mercifully to accept this our sacrifice of praise and thanksgiving."

Whether or not we choose to refer to the Lord's table as the altar, it is certainly the Lord's *table*. The trend in recent years is once again toward a table that looks like a table. Even churches and great cathedrals that have ornate and historic altars fixed against the wall now often have, in addition, a free-standing table at which Holy Communion is actually celebrated and served. A number of United Methodist churches that once had Communion tables and then put in an altar against the wall a generation or so ago have now discovered their old Communion table (often in some classroom) and have placed it, free-standing, in front of the fixed altar.

If you are making or buying a new table, it should be free-standing, with enough open space around it so that persons can walk around it and the minister can stand behind it to preside in Christ's name at the Lord's Supper. Since it is not a table to be sat around, a counter height of thirty-nine inches, rather than the usual thirty-inch dining table height, will function better. This height makes it easier for the minister to stand behind the table, read the service, and handle the bread and cup. A width of twenty-four inches and a length of at least five feet are also customary and practical for the serving of Communion.

In the following chapters we shall consider in detail what is appropriate on or around the Lord's table, but certain principles are crucial: (1) nothing should detract from the primary function of the table, which is to be the place where the Lord's Supper is celebrated; (2) everything used on the table should be selected and procured with great care and be appropriate to its holy purpose; (3) everything should express to the worshiper the qualities of truth, integrity, simplicity,

21

and purity. Anything that expresses falseness or pretence, or that is gaudy or cheaply ornate, should be avoided.

This principle of integrity is not a matter of rigid rules as to what is "correct," nor does it mean that what is more costly or more beautiful is necessarily better. Often the worth of an article is more to be found in the quality of work and material involved than in the dollars-and-cents cost. A cheaper material that is genuine is more appropriate than an imitation of a more expensive material. We express outwardly, by our use of material things, what we are inwardly. What we see sometimes "speaks" so loudly that it cancels out what we hear, and the sloppy appearance of the chancel can make it harder to hear the preaching of Christian commitment and consecration. On the other hand, this message is powerfully reinforced when the worshipers see before them visual evidence that there are people who care enough to give their best.

[SYMBOLS]

Your congregation in its worship constantly uses symbols, and as you prepare the environment for worship you will constantly be using symbols. We have seen in the previous chapter that the space and furnishings used in worship are symbols—that is, they represent something beyond themselves, usually something abstract or immaterial. Words are symbols, acts can be symbols, and there are countless visual symbols.

It is with these visual symbols that this chapter is concerned. Look carefully around the place where your congregation worships and notice the great number of pictures and designs that are used in the chancel appointments, the stained-glass windows, the woodwork, the walls and ceiling, hymnals and bulletins. Their purpose is not to be admired as an end in themselves but rather to lead us beyond themselves to God. Most of us learn even more through our eyes than through our ears, and we are familiar with the truth of the old Chinese proverb that "a picture is worth ten thousand words." The language of the Bible is filled with vivid word-pictures that have inspired Christian art since ancient times.

The most familiar symbol of our Christian faith is the cross. Jesus Christ gave us life by dying on a cross and rising from the dead. Long before the time of Christ, pre-Christian peoples used the cross as a symbol of life; and it was natural for Christians to see in the cross not only a symbol of how Jesus Christ died but also of the life he gives us.

Because the cross is so rich in its symbolism, Christians have used many forms of the cross. Sometimes the cross has Christ hanging from it (a crucifix), and we are reminded of his suffering and death. Most commonly in our churches the cross is empty, reminding us that he is no longer on the cross but is risen. Sometimes the cross has on it the figure of Christ reigning and exalted, signifying that Christ lives and reigns today and will come again in final victory. The empty cross itself comes in various shapes, each with its distinctive symbolic emphasis.

Here are some of the most common forms.

Latin Cross, the one used by the Romans to put Jesus to death and the most commonly used form in chancels.

Greek Cross, with four arms of equal length.

Celtic Cross, with a circle symbolizing eternity.

Budded Cross, with trefoil ends symbolic of life and of the Trinity.

Saint Andrew's Cross, so called because Saint Andrew is said to have died on such a cross.

Jerusalem Cross, symbolizing the spread of the gospel from Jerusalem to the four corners of the earth.

Maltese Cross, whose spreading arms and eight points symbolize human regeneration and the eight beatitudes.

Tau Cross, so named because it is shaped like the Greek letter tau, the equivalent of our "T."

There are many other forms of the cross and a great many Christian symbols other than the cross—so many that every church library or Altar Guild ought to have a reference book on Christian symbols. See the bibliography. Such a book will enable you not only to identify and explain the symbols now in your church but also to do more creative designing in the future.

Here are a few of the symbols most commonly found in chancels.

Triangle, a symbol of the Trinity.

Trefoil, a symbol of the Trinity.

Fleur-de-lis, a symbol of the Trinity.

Three Intertwined Circles, a symbol of the Trinity.

26

Triquetra, a symbol of the Trinity. The three equal arcs represent eternity in their continuous form and indivisibility in their interweaving. Their center is a triangle, itself a symbol of the Trinity.

All-seeing Eye of God, which looks out from the triangle of the Trinity.

Alpha and Omega, the first and last letters of the Greek alphabet, used to represent our Lord. "I am the Alpha and the Omega, the first and the last, the beginning and the end" (Rev. 22:13).

Open Bible, symbolizing the Word of God.

IHS, the first three letters of the name "Jesus" in Greek, used as a monogram to signify Jesus.

Chi Rho, the first two letters in the Greek word for "Christ," superimposed on one another to signify Christ.

INRI, the initial letters for the Latin inscription on the cross: Iesus Nazarenus, Rex Iudaeorum (Jesus of Nazareth, King of the Jews—John 19:19), used as a symbol for Jesus.

Fish, drawn by early Christians in the days of persecution to identify one another. The initial letters of the Greek words "Jesus Christ, Son of God, Savior" make the word for "fish" in Greek.

Hand of God, symbol of the Father, as Blesser. The three extended fingers suggest the Trinity, while the two closed fingers symbolize the twofold nature of the Son.

Rose, symbolizing the Nativity of our Lord, or Mary his mother.

Descending Dove, represents the Holy Spirit and has its origin in the account of our Lord's baptism (Matt. 3:16).

Shell with Drops of Water, symbolizes baptism.

28

Cup, represents the blood of Christ and the Sacrament of Holy Communion. Sometimes combined with a loaf of bread, a wafer, or a cross.

Crown of Thorns and Nails, symbolize our Lord's Passion.

The Lamb Standing with the Banner of Victory, symbolizing the victorious nature of Jesus' sacrifice (Rev. 17:14).

Cross and Crown, symbolize the reward of the faithful after death and also that there is no crown without a cross.

Butterfly, symbolizes the resurrection.

Anchor, symbolizes hope.

Two Intertwined Rings, a symbol of marriage.

Winged Man, represents Matthew the Evangelist, because his Gospel traces Jesus' genealogy.

Winged Lion, represents Mark the Evangelist, because his Gospel begins, "The voice of one crying in the wilderness," and this suggests the roar of a lion.

Winged Ox, represents Luke the Evangelist, because the ox is the animal of sacrifice and Luke stresses the atoning sacrifice of Christ.

Winged Eagle, represents John the Evangelist, because in his Gospel he rises to loftiest heights in dealing with the mind of Christ.

Shepherd, symbolizes the loving care of Jesus, the Good Shepherd.

Ship, symbolizes the church. The word "nave" comes from the Latin word for "ship."

Trumpet, symbolizes the day of judgment and the resurrection.

Scales of justice.

Jesse Tree, derived from Isaiah 11:1.

Gifts of the Wise Men.

Palm Leaf, used at Jesus' entry into Jerusalem, is a symbol of victory.

Crown of Thorns, a mockery, symbol of Jesus' humiliation and suffering (John 19:2).

Scourge and Pillar symbolize Jesus' suffering.

Ladder Crossed with Reed and Sponge, symbolizing our Lord's crucifixion, since the sponge was used to provide him vinegar while on the cross (Matt. 27:48).

Three Nails, driven through the palms and feet at his crucifixion and symbols of his suffering.

Crowing Cock, warning and rebuking Peter (Mark 14:72).

Money Bag and Silver Coins, symbolizing the treachery of Judas (Matt. 26:15).

Phoenix, a mythical bird that at death bursts into flame but rises from its own ashes, symbolizing the resurrection.

Peacock, symbolizng the resurrection. When it loses its feathers, it grows more brilliant ones than those it lost.

Bursting Pomegranate, symbolizing the resurrection and the power of our Lord, who was able to burst the tomb and come forth.

Downward Arrow, symbolizing the descent of the Holy Spirit.

Lamp, symbolizing the Word of God (Ps. 119:105).

Epiphany Star (Matt. 2:1-2).

[VESTING FOR WORSHIP]

We began by considering the room and furniture that form the basic environment of congregational worship, but this environment seems bare if it is not somehow adorned for worship—decorated so as to look festive, or somber, or whatever is appropriate to worship on a particular occasion. The ancient Jews richly adorned the temple in Jerusalem, and as soon as the early Christians were able to set aside space especially for worship they began to "vest" this space. The verb "to vest" comes from the Latin word *vestire*, which means to clothe for the purpose of exhibiting authority. To vest a person means to give that person an article of clothing that designates certain rights and responsibilities. When people vest for worship they put on garments that signify their function in that worship. To vest the space or furnishings used for worship means to clothe them with material that signifies their holy function.

Vesting the Place of Worship

There is no one and only correct way to vest a Christian place of worship, no authority that has made rules that we must follow. As you go from church to church and denomination to denomination you will see a wide variety of styles. There is much room for the exercise of creativity and imagination.

On the other hand, there are ancient traditions that tie us with Christians of many times and places, and there is a growing consensus in many denominations that helps us adapt these ancient traditions so that we can identify with them today.

You probably have among your duties the care of what are commonly called the "altar cloths."

Since Old Testament times persons have expressed their devotion to God by artistry in fabrics that were given to be used in places of worship. In the account of the tabernacle we read: "All women who had ability spun with their hands, and brought what they had spun in blue and purple and scarlet stuff and fine twined linen" (Exod. 35:25).

Christians from early times have covered the Lord's table with fine cloths that signify this table's very special and holy purpose. We are accustomed to covering our dining tables with tablecloths, especially for a festive meal; and it is only natural that we should make or seek out the finest of cloths to cover the table that is reserved for the Holy Meal. The traditional altar cloths include linens and paraments. Linens are usually white, and paraments are in colors signifying the day or season of the Christian year.

Linens

The Lord's table is traditionally covered with three white linen cloths. They signify that this is the table of

the Lord and should be in place at all times, except on
Good Friday, whether or not Holy Communion is
being celebrated.

1. The first linen to be placed is a foundation cloth
of coarse linen, called a cerecloth, exactly the size of
the top ("mensa") of the table. It is plainly hemmed
and may be waxed to prevent dampness from staining
the other cloths, especially if the mensa is of stone. If
the mensa is of wood, as is generally the case in United
Methodist churches, the cerecloth is less necessary
and is often omitted.

2. The second linen is placed over the cerecloth and
is attached to the paraments, which will be discussed
below. Its purpose is to hold the paraments in place,
and since it is not seen it may also be a coarse linen. It is
the same depth as the mensa and the same width as
the parament. Sometimes the parament itself is
constructed so as to cover the mensa and form this
second layer of cloth. When there are no paraments,
this second layer of cloth may be omitted.

3. The top linen is a very fine quality of plain white
linen and is traditionally called the "fair linen." It is
usually the same depth as the mensa, but its length
may vary. It may be the same length as the mensa, or it
may extend over the ends of the mensa either
one-third or two-thirds of the height of the table.

This "fair linen" is what is referred by the
Communion Ritual in *The Book of Hymns* and *The Book
of Worship*, which specifies that "at the time of Holy
Communion, the Lord's Table shall have upon it a fair
white linen cloth." Even if the two lower linens are
omitted, the fair linen should be in place, at least when
Holy Communion is being celebrated. When Holy

Communion is not being celebrated the use of the fair linen on the Lord's table is optional but has much to be said for it as a reminder of the nature and function of the Lord's table.

The Altar Linens

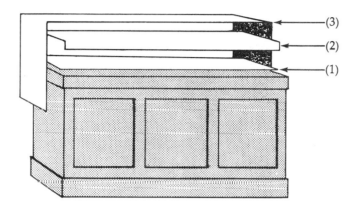

(1) *Foundation cloth*　　　(2) *Second linen*　　　(3) *Fair linen*

The tradition of referring to this as the *fair* linen indicates that this linen should not only be of the finest quality but also has been prepared and made beautiful for a special purpose. The word "fair" is used here to mean "free from blemish, imperfection, or anything that impairs the appearance, quality, or character." The fair linen should always be spotless and should never be folded. A church should own at least two fair linens, so that one is always in reserve. The fair linen may be covered with a protector cloth of cotton or linen, or even white or clear plastic, when the church is not open for public or private worship, but these should always be removed during services.

When Holy Communion is celebrated, some churches use additional fair linens to cover the bread and the cup. If the bread and cups are in trays with a lid, these trays or stacks of trays do not need a linen cover. If there are no lids, the bread and cup may be covered with small linen cloths, or a linen-covered square of stiff cardboard or other lightweight material may be placed on the cup, or there may be no covering. If covered bread and wine are already in place on the Lord's table during the first part of the service, they are uncovered at the offering. Coverings are unnecessary if the bread and wine are brought to the Lord's table at the offering.

If a common chalice is used, there should also be several small linen napkins (called purificators) to wipe the rim of the chalice(s) as people drink or to catch any dripping if the bread is dipped into the chalice. These are usually twelve to fifteen inches square and are folded when not in use.

If you make your own fair linens, here are some practical suggestions:

1. Since linen shrinks somewhat, be sure it is pre-shrunk before it is cut to size.

2. Hand-hem the fair linen that covers the mensa with a one-inch hem on the sides and a three-inch hem on the ends, with mitered corners. Hemming should be on the straight of the material which can be determined by pulling a thread. Slip stitch with linen thread or waxed mercerized cotton thread, catching one thread of the top layer as you hem and stitching as close together as possible. The stitching should be

almost invisible on the right side. Hemstitching is not recommended, as it will wear out much sooner.

3. Lace edges are not appropriate for the fair linen.

The maintenance of the linens is a responsibility that must not be neglected. Here are some guidelines:

1. Launder the Communion linens after each use and the other linens at least once a month and whenever they become soiled or dusty, so that the linens on the Lord's table are always spotless.

2. Do not send them to a commercial laundry or cleaner or launder them in a load with other items. Use only a mild unscented soap. Never use bleach, blueing, or starch. You may wish to soak them in cold water before washing. After washing, rinse them thoroughly several times.

3. To remove wax drippings: (a) scrape with a blunt instrument, (b) then place a blotter or absorbent brown wrapping paper under the linen, (c) then press over the spot with a hot iron until the wax disappears. Keep the candle snuffers clean to prevent black wax spots.

4. Lipstick stains on purificators and some wine (grape juice) stains can be removed by lengthy soaking followed by a thorough rubbing with a mild soap solution. More stubborn wine stains may be removed by placing the linen over a bowl and pouring boiling water through the stain until it fades from view. The sooner stains are treated, the easier they are to remove.

5. Do not wring them but roll them in towels to remove excess water. Iron while still quite damp, first on the wrong side and then on the right side. Be sure that they are perfectly dry before rolling or folding

them for storage, or else they will be uneven and rippled. Fold by hand after ironing, not with the iron itself.

6. Do not fold the fair and protector linens but roll them on heavy tubes and wrap them in tissue paper for storage. Store smaller linens flat in clean drawers.

Paraments

Paraments are hangings of fine cloth, traditionally silk, which decorate the Lord's table, the pulpit, and the lectern (if there is one). Their colors signify the day or season of the Christian year and their symbols represent various aspects of the Christian faith. As such, they are powerful devotional and educational tools, and they have been so used since the sixth century A.D.

The four basic colors of paraments are red, white, purple, and green. Other colors may also be appropriate. Suggestions for parament colors and symbols are found below in the chapter on the Christian year.

There are four types of paraments for the Lord's table.

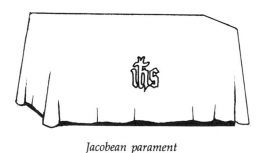

Jacobean parament

1. The Jacobean (or Laudean) parament is thrown over the table and covers all four sides, hanging in folds at the corners. Since this requires a free-standing table, it has been used in those periods of church history when the table was free-standing and for this reason is increasingly used today.

Full frontal

2. The full frontal covers the entire front of the table and is often used when the table is plain.

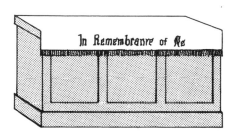

Superfrontal

3. The superfrontal is a frontal which extends the length of the table but hangs down only six to twelve inches. It may hang in front of a full frontal, or it may be used by itself when the table is ornate.

41

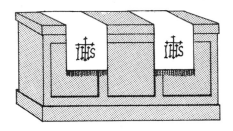

Frontlets

4. Frontlets, also known as altar stoles or antependia, are strips that hang from the front of the table, or from both front and back, about three-fourths of the distance to the floor. These may be appropriate in rare situations when the table is particularly fine or ornate.

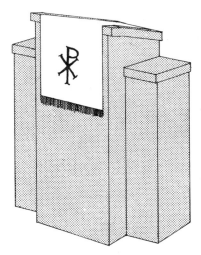

Pulpit frontal

42

Paraments in front of the pulpit and lectern (if there is one) are known as antependia, frontals, or falls. They are usually suspended from a piece of cloth attached to the top of the pulpit or lectern. They usually match the altar paraments in color and fabric, but the symbols may complement.

Sometimes one or two Bible markers are hung in front of the pulpit or lectern. If, as is commonly the case, they are not actually used to mark the Bible they violate the principle of integrity. For both symbolic and practical reasons, it is better that the Bible itself be plainly seen by the congregation and that the markers not be visible to them.

While many churches order paraments either ready-made or made to order from church supply houses or professional designers, members of many other churches make their own paraments. They do not have to be of traditional silk or damask. Texture, color, shape, and design can be chosen to blend with the architecture and existing decor and signify the day, season, or other special emphasis. They may be traditional, with intricate stitching and ornate design, gold braid and fringe on rich dark colors. They may strike the contemporary notes of simplicity and strength, vibrancy and celebration.

Maintenance of the paraments, like that of the linens, is a responsibility that must not be neglected. Paraments need cleaning less often than linens, but they usually require dry cleaning by experts. If paraments are purchased, instructions for cleaning them may be included and should be kept for reference. Paraments should be inspected for soiling and should always be spotless. This is especially the case with white paraments.

Paraments may be stored flat in clean drawers, or by hanging over rods in special cabinets. They should never be folded, since this eventually harms the fabric.

Lenten Veils

In many churches crosses and pictures which express Christian joy and victory are covered on Good Friday, or during Holy Week, or throughout Lent, to stress the solemnity of the day or season. The veil for the cross may be made from mesh or cheesecloth dyed purple or blue or gray and may be gathered at the base with thread. Pictures and other symbols of joy may be veiled with unbleached linen.

Banners

Banners have been used in churches since ancient times, but for a long time they were rare, and only in the last generation have they become widely popular. Their simple, bold colors and designs seem especially well-suited to contemporary Christian feelings and tastes. While they can be purchased, they are generally made and donated by church members.

Banners can be used in various ways. They can be hung on poles, carried in the procession, placed in stands during the service, and then carried out in the recession. They can be hung from the ceiling, the balcony, or from poles perpendicular to the walls. They can be directly hung on walls and columns. Banners are most effective when they highlight the day or season being celebrated, a special emphasis or a particular event in the church, or some timeless Christian affirmation or theme.

Because they have been so fashionable in recent years, they have often been carelessly and ineffectively used in ways that have caused people to react against them. Here are some suggestions:

1. Banners should be in good taste, express some aspect of the Christian gospel, and contribute to the spirit of worship.
2. It should be understood that no one banner is a permanent fixture in the church but is for use on one or more particular occasions or seasons.
3. Banners should be simple in design and not attract undue attention to themselves.
4. Most of the best banners do not use words. If words are used, they should be few and subordinate in the overall design.
5. A banner should be hung properly, centered in its space, and be an appropriate size so it is framed by its background.
6. No banner should hide or distract from the cross or the basic chancel furnishings.
7. Keep banners well away from open flames, high intensity lights, or heating or cooling vents.
8. If a banner is kept to be used again, it should be stored in a straight box or hung on hangers with plastic coverings. Do not wrinkle fringes, and be prepared to iron out any wrinkles before using again. Do not use a soiled or dingy banner, or one that is visibly in need of repair.
9. The pastor has the final responsibility in the selection and use of banners, as in all else relating

to the environment and conduct of congregational worship.

Vesting the People

The way those in leadership roles dress when the congregation comes together for worship is an important part of the environment of that worship and has its impact on each worshiper just as surely as does the way the room and its furnishings are vested.

Of course, your responsibilities in this area are probably very limited. People wear what they wish when they come to worship. The choir and instrumentalists, if they wear robes or vestments or other special dress of any kind, probably take responsibility themselves to select, procure, and maintain what they wear. The minister or ministers probably have selected and own what they wish to wear and take the responsibility for maintaining it.

On the other hand, you may be given responsibilities for the cleaning and storage of these vestments. You may be called on for advice or assistance because of your expertise in fabrics or sewing. The ministerial stole, in particular, is often bought or made to match the paraments. So it is helpful for you to know something about vestments.

Most United Methodist ministers who wear vestments wear either an academic robe or an alb.

The academic robe (traditionally black but now sometimes white or some other color) developed from the academic dress of medieval universities as the uniform of scholars. It is sometimes worn with an academic hood, which indicates the wearer's degree.

46

If the wearer has a doctor's degree, the robe may be the doctor's robe with three sleeve stripes. Since this reflects secular use and emphasizes distinctions in the educational achievements of ministers, such garb is increasingly considered inappropriate for worship except in academic settings.

Academic robe

The alb is the oldest Christian vestment and was part of the everyday dress worn by Roman men and women. After it passed out of style in the secular world about A.D. 400, it continued to be used as a worship vestment. In recent years it has become ecumenically the most widely accepted basic worship vestment.

The name of the garment comes from its color—*alba*, which means "white" in Latin. Albs are always white, off-white, flaxen, or (for penitential seasons) ash-gray. It has traditionally never been a colored garment.

47

Cassock alb   Chasuble alb

All participants in the service, lay or ordained, may wear the alb, since it does not signify either ordination or academic achievement but unites us with the everyday dress of the early Christians and with the church of all times and places. It is increasingly worn today by ministers, by choirs, and by laypersons who take leadership roles in worship.

It may be worn either with or without a belt, called a cincture, which is either a tassled rope or a cloth band about four inches wide.

Generally speaking, albs are washable, whereas academic robes must be professionally dry-cleaned.

United Methodist ministers today also commonly wear stoles, which are a badge of ordination indicating the one who has been called to lead the community in the sacramental life of the church. Stoles developed from the silk scarf worn by ancient Roman officials as a badge of office. They should not be worn by non-ordained persons.

Stoles are long, narrow bands of heavy silk or other fabric worn around the neck, over the shoulders, and extending to the knees. They are usually the color of the day or season of the Christian year, sometimes have symbols embroidered on them, and are often designed to be used with a matching set of paraments. They are often worn over academic robes but are traditionally associated with albs and are more appropriately worn over an alb. They should be in keeping with the overall design of the vestments with which they are used.

Deacon's stole   Elder's stole

Deacons have traditionally worn the stole over the left shoulder to indicate the difference in their role from that of the elder. The deacon's stole may be fastened at the bottom with a simple snap or hook.

Stoles, like academic robes and albs, may be purchased from church supply houses; but they are often made and presented to a minister by church members.

[Worship Appointments]

In addition to the basic furnishings and the coverings with which they are vested, the chancel is furnished with various ornaments and appointments which serve both practical and symbolic functions. Some are always used, and others are used only at certain times of the year. They may be purchased or crafted by creative persons. It is important that they be selected and placed so as to enhance the congregation's worship, and the Altar Guild or its equivalent in your church can play a key role in seeing that this is done.

The Cross

It is customary that there be one large symbol of Christ near the Lord's table. This can be a tapestry, painting, sculpture, or mosaic of Christ. Most commonly, however, it is a large cross. This central symbol of Christ should be more prominent in size and construction than any of the other appointments. If it is a cross, it may be fastened to the "east" wall of the chancel (see illustration on page 14) or be suspended from the ceiling above the Lord's table. In either case it can easily be of appropriate size and prominence without interfering with the setting and functioning of the Lord's table.

It may stand on the retable behind the Lord's table. A cross in that location, however, is rarely large and prominent enough in relation to the rest of the chancel and its appointments to signify effectively the centrality of what the cross stands for in our faith.

The cross should not be placed on the Lord's table itself. This unfortunate placement originated when the medieval priests placed a cross, invisible to the congregation, before them on the altar as an object of private devotion. In such a position it interferes with the placement and use of the Communion bread and cup, and if the table is free-standing it makes it very awkward for the minister to stand behind the table facing the people.

Some churches weaken the symbolism of the cross in their chancels by having two crosses. One, for example, may be on the retable and the other on the wall above the retable. This redundancy makes for uncertainty as to what is the visual focus of the chancel and keeps the eye of the worshiper from centering attention on one cross. If you now have two crosses in the vicinity of the Lord's table, it would be much better to find another more suitable place for whichever of them—probably the smaller one on the table or retable—is the less prominent. There is very likely some chapel or devotional center elsewhere in the church where that cross would be most effective and appropriate.

A processional cross is a cross at the top of a pole or shaft carried in procession, placed in a stand during the service, and carried out in the recession. Processional crosses, which have been used since the fourth century, are a much older tradition than altar crosses. If a processional cross is used in a church which has another cross near the altar, it should not be placed so near the other cross during the service that there is the redundancy effect mentioned above.

Candles

Candles have been used in Christian worship since ancient times, first because they provided the light necessary for reading and in recent times simply for their symbolic value, signifying Christ as the light of the world (John 8:12; 12:46).

The most traditional of candles in Christian worship is the Paschal Candle, a large decorative candle symbolic of Christ's appearances following his resurrection. It is lighted at the beginning of the Easter Vigil (Easter Eve or the first service of Easter) and carried in procession to the vicinity of the Lord's table, where it is placed in its special stand and where it remains and is lighted at each service until the Day of Pentecost. It is then placed near the baptismal font for the rest of the year and lighted whenever there is a baptism. (See illustration on page 54.) It may be carried at the head of funeral processions. The Paschal Candle should be at least two inches in diameter and at least two feet tall. Its holder should be at least three feet high. As part of the Easter Vigil each year, the new Paschal Candle may be inscribed with a cross, the Greek letters *alpha* and *omega*, and the numerals of the current year.

Grains of incense and five wax nails may be inserted into the cross.

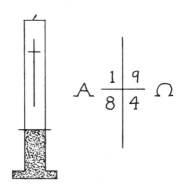

Paschal candle and inscription

The most commonly used candles are altar candles, which were originally needed to provide light to read the service. These should be placed on the retable or, if the Lord's table is free-standing, in floor-standing holders at the corners or on either side of the table. Since nothing should overshadow the cross, the candle flames should never be higher than the arms of the cross. This is no problem if the cross is hanging or fastened to the wall, and in traditional retables the problem is averted by a raised platform in the center of the retable on which the cross stands.

In many churches these altar candles are placed on the Lord's table itself, but this causes practical and symbolic problems. In the first place, unless the candles are very short and in very low holders, they so dominate the table that they violate the principle that nothing should detract from the primary function of the table as the place where the Lord's Supper is celebrated. Problems are compounded if, as is often the case, the cross as well as the candles sits on the Lord's table itself. The total effect of cross and candles tends to detract all the more from the primary function of the Lord's table, and since the cross stands on the same level as the candles it may be hard to keep them below the arms of the cross.

Another problem in placing candles on the Lord's table itself is the danger of wax dripping on the fair linen. The problem is even more acute in those churches that do not use a fair linen except when there is Communion and where hard-to-clean parament cloth itself covers the top of the table. Some churches try to deal with the problem by placing heavy transparent plastic or some similar protective covering over the top of the table, or at least a square of it under each candle; but this seriously detracts from the appearance of the table.

Sometimes a distinction is made between "altar candles" on the Lord's table and "office lights" placed behind or beside the Lord's table, but since either can be lighted for any or all services in present-day usage there is no particular reason to make such a distinction.

Many churches use additional candles or candelabra, especially at night, for festive occasions such as Christmas and Easter and for weddings and other special occasions. These should stand either on the floor or on the retable.

The manner of lighting and extinguishing candles can significantly add to, or detract from, the worship. If someone strolls down the aisle at the last moment and strikes a match or uses a cigarette lighter, this hardly adds to the spirit of worship. On the other hand, a trained acolyte, using a candle lighter and extinguisher, can reverently light the candles at the beginning of the service and extinguish them after the benediction as an integral part of the congregation's worship. While the training and use of acolytes is outside the scope of this book, you or others in your church should consider an acolyte program if you do not already have one. Resources are suggested in the bibliography.

Sometimes large candles attached to wooden or metal shafts are carried in processions just behind the processional cross and then, like the processional cross, placed in stands in the chancel. These processional torches, as they are called, symbolize the coming of Christ to lighten the darkness of the world and should be reserved for high festival occasions.

A few United Methodist churches have sanctuary lamps or "eternal lights"—suspended from the ceiling or mounted on the wall near the Lord's table—which burn continuously through the week. In Roman Catholic tradition they signify the presence of Christ in the reserved sacrament; in Protestant tradition they signify Christ's presence in the church.

Candles used in church should be at least 51 percent beeswax so that they will burn evenly. Candle caps will both keep the wax from dripping down the sides of the candles and also lengthen the life of the candles. Electric or battery-powered lights that look like candles violate the principle of integrity in worship; they appear to be what they are not.

Many churches hold candlelighting ceremonies on such occasions as Christmas Eve or the Easter Vigil, where every member of the congregation is given a small candle and where at a given point in the service the candles are all lighted. These services are very popular and impressive but require precautions. Some fire inspectors discourage or forbid such services. In addition to danger from hand-held flames there is the danger of dripping hot wax, especially if the candles are not stuck into cardboard protectors. If your church holds such services be *sure* that fire extinguishers are available and that the ushers are prepared for any emergency.

Other Altarware

Several other items of altarware are in common use, and you will probably be responsible for their maintenance.

Churches commonly have *flower vases* that match or coordinate with the altar cross and candlesticks. More will be said about flowers below.

Candle lighter and extinguisher

Candle lighters and extinguishers have already been mentioned. There may be one or two of them, depending on whether your church uses one or two acolytes. They should match or coordinate with the candlesticks.

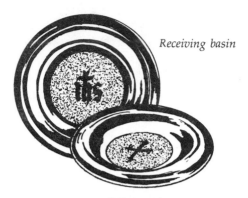

Receiving basin

Offering plate

Offering plates are also often bought to match or coordinate with the other altarware. When the offering is brought forward during the service, these plates are received at the altar and are sometimes stacked in a large matching *receiving basin.* Many churches place the filled offering plates on the Lord's table, but these plates are often so conspicuous that they violate the principle that nothing should detract from the primary function of the table as the place where Holy Communion is celebrated. It is more appropriate to place the filled plates on a side table or shelf in the chancel, or possibly on the retable. Some churches use baskets or alms bags in place of offering plates, and to place them on the Lord's table would be even more inappropriate. In any event, plates, baskets, or bags should never be placed on the Lord's table when they are empty but should be kept either on a side table or shelf in the chancel or in the back of the church.

Some churches have a *missal stand* or *missal pillow,* which holds the service book on the table at a suitable angle and distance for easy reading by the minister. Because the key prayers at Holy Communion are usually read and the minister's hands must be free, it is appropriate and necessary that the printed service be placed on the Lord's table during Holy Communion, but the placement should be such that it in no way interferes with the centrality of the bread and cup or lessens their visual prominence.

At this point it is important to correct a common misunderstanding. A missal stand is *not* a Bible stand, and the practice of placing an open Bible on a stand on the Lord's table or the retable so it faces the people confuses the functions of pulpit and table. The pulpit (or possibly the lectern) is the place from which the Scriptures are "opened" to the people by reading and preaching and therefore the place on which an open Bible is an appropriate and powerful symbol. An open Bible on the Lord's table detracts from the function of the table as the place where Holy Communion is celebrated. Furthermore, this practice violates the principle of integrity by placing the Bible permanently where it cannot be used. As James F. White once said to me: "When I see an open Bible on the Lord's table I immediately know two things: first, that this Bible is *not* going to be read and, second, that today on this table the Lord's Supper is *not* going to be celebrated."

Altarware Maintenance

One of your most important responsibilities is the maintenance of the altarware. These objects have been consecrated to the worship of God and should be both reverently handled and carefully maintained. Here are some suggestions:

1. Wearing soft cotton gloves while handling altarware keeps the moisture and oiliness of skin from tarnishing the metal or marking the candles.

2. Since altarware is made in a variety of metals and other materials, obtain instructions for its care and cleaning from the manufacturer. If this is not possible, you may follow the guidelines given below.

3. Determine whether or not any brass ware has been lacquered to prevent tarnishing.

a. If it has, clean by wiping with a soft damp cloth and then immediately dry with a clean soft cloth. Never immerse in water, touch with detergents or abrasives, or polish, as these procedures will severely damage the lacquer. When the lacquer begins to wear or peel, have the item relacquered by a jeweler or by the manufacturer.

b. Unlacquered brass must never be touched with bare hands or damp cloths, since these cause tarnishing. Rinse in very hot water and dry with paper towels or soft cloth. Too much polishing is not good for brass; two or three times a year with a fine grade of metal polish is enough. Maintain shine in the interim by rubbing with a soft cloth or treated polishing gloves.

4. Wash silver altarware in hot soapy water, rinse in clear hot water, and dry immediately. Polish two or three times a year with a fine grade of silver polish. Never allow polish to dry on the surface. Maintain shine in the interim as with unlacquered brass.

5. When altarware is not in use, store in clean cotton flannel bags to prevent tarnishing. Have a place for each item, keep each one in its proper place, and label each one to prevent unnecessary handling.

6. Candles and candleholders need special care

because of wax drippings. Never scratch with fingernails or any other instrument, since this will leave marks, but use a soft dry cloth to remove wax drippings. Peel wax drippings off the sides of the candles themselves when the wax is completely cold. Hold the candles themselves in a clean cloth so as not to leave finger marks.

7. Candles can be cleaned with alcohol or salad oil on a very soft cloth and shined with a piece of nylon stocking.

8. Because candles harden with age, older candles burn longer. If they are ordered in quantity to allow aging, they must be kept in a cool place, the cooler the better.

9. New candlewicks will be easier for acolytes to light and less likely to sputter out if they are lighted for a few minutes when new. Long candle wicks need trimming to keep the charred ends from breaking off and soiling linens. If the wick is short, carve the candle down enough to facilitate lighting.

10. Candle caps need to be removed and cleaned from time to time. Remove the cap from the candle while the wax is still warm, wipe away excess wax from it, and trim the candle to expose the wick.

11. Candle lighters and extinguishers also need special care. Any soot accumulation in the bell top is a potential hazard to linens, rugs, and floors and can be removed with hot water and paper towels.

Flowers

Flowers speak of festivity, and to Christians flowers speak specifically of the resurrection. Flowers given to the church can be an exquisite offering of praise and thanksgiving, and they are also a fitting way of memorializing loved ones in worship on the anniversary of their death or birth. It is not surprising that flowers have become such a favorite means of decorating the environment of worship.

They can, however, easily be misused and fail to contribute as they should to the environment of worship. Here are some suggestions:

1. Flowers should be in keeping with the architecture and other decorations of the church, large and colorful enough to be seen from the back pews and in harmony with the color scheme of the church and of the day or season. Smaller arrangements and pastel colors are best suited to a small space such as a chapel or prayer room.

2. Do not overdo the flowers. They are not a florist's display and should blend in with the environment of worship rather than dominating it. The most expressive floral arrangements are likely to be very simple.

3. The overall effect of the church decorations, including flowers, should always lead the eye to the Lord's table and the cross. Flowers may be placed on floor stands or some other suitable location, but they should never obscure the cross or the Lord's table or rise above the arms of the cross.

4. Do not place flowers on the Lord's table, as this practice detracts from the primary purpose of the table as the place where Holy Communion is celebrated.

5. Do not create a fire hazard by placing flowers or greenery too near candles.

6. Do not use anything that is likely to wilt or otherwise deteriorate before the end of the service. If

flowers are left after the services, they should be checked each day that the church is open and removed immediately when they have passed their prime.

7. Since flowers symbolize the resurrection, and in keeping with the principle of integrity, no type of artificial flower or plant is appropriate to the environment of worship. If for a given service no fresh flowers are available, there are several alternatives. One is to use evergreens or mixed greenery. Another alternative is to have one or more sets of potted plants available for use whenever needed. Still another alternative is to use no flowers or greenery; this makes them appreciated more when they *are* available and is especially appropriate during a more somber season such as Lent.

8. Flower vases or containers should be attractive and in harmony with their environment and large and heavy enough to be in good proportion. Be sure that potted plants are not placed where they may cause stains. The vases or containers should be stored when the flowers are gone. Empty vases should never remain in the chancel.

9. It is not in good taste to use symbols or ribbons in floral arrangements.

10. You may wish to create your own floral arrangements for the church rather than rely on florists. Floral art is interpretive design, using color and form. It is a liturgical art and a beautiful way of making worship offerings to God. Recommended resources are listed in the bibliography.

11. After services, flowers may be taken to the sick.

[The Christian Year]

As you work to prepare the environment for worship week in and week out, be aware of the traditional calendar of days and seasons that your church observes each year. Some of these are purely local, like an anniversary or a homecoming. Others are set by your Annual Conference or by denominational agencies, perhaps to promote some particular cause. Still others, and these are the most basic ones, have been observed by Christians of many denominations, have centuries of custom and tradition behind them, and constitute what is commonly called the Christian year.

Some observances in the Christian year such as Christmas and Easter are well known to all of us; others are less well known. Some are confusing because different denominations have observed them differently or because different reference books give conflicting information about them. The Christian year has a complicated and fascinating history, which you may wish to study using the books listed in the bibliography. The Christian year is also closely related to the lectionary, a three-year cycle of Scripture readings recommended for public worship by many denominations around the world. If your minister uses the lectionary, you may wish to study it.

What follows is the Common Calendar of the Christian year as agreed upon in 1978 and 1982 by representatives of the major North American denominations. It is based on the oldest Christian traditions and is essentially the calendar that is used by the vast majority of Christians around the world. It starts with Advent, which is the beginning of the Christian year. The seasons are given in capital letters, and the Sundays and other special days are given in lower case. With this calendar a simple sequence of colors is suggested for your paraments, for the minister's stole, and perhaps for other decorations as well. A short statement is then made about each of the basic colors. These color suggestions are based on historic and common usage, but there has been and still is among Christians variation in the use of colors.

The final section of this chapter gives additional visual suggestions—colors, textures, and symbols—to stimulate the imagination of those who, with qualified guidance, wish to be creative.

The Calendar

ADVENT—from Sunday November 27 or the first Sunday after November 27 to sunset December 24, always including four Sundays
First through Fourth Sunday in Advent—*Purple*

CHRISTMAS SEASON—from sunset December 24 through January 6
Christmas Eve and Christmas Day—December 25—*White*

*First and Second Sunday after Christmas—*White*
Epiphany—January 6 or first Sunday in January—
White

SEASON AFTER EPIPHANY—from January 7
through day before Lent
First Sunday after Epiphany, or the Baptism of the
Lord—*White*
*Second through next-to-last Sunday after
Epiphany—*Green*
Last Sunday after Epiphany, or the Transfiguration
—*White*

LENT—from the seventh Wednesday before Easter to
sunset Easter Eve
Ash Wednesday (first day of Lent)—*Purple*
First through Fifth Sunday in Lent—*Purple*
Passion/Palm Sunday (Sixth Sunday in Lent)—
Purple
Monday, Tuesday, and Wednesday in Holy Week—
Purple
Maundy (Holy) Thursday—*Purple*
Good Friday and Holy Saturday—*No Color*

EASTER SEASON—from sunset Easter Eve through
the Day of Pentecost
Easter Eve and Easter Day—*White*
Second through Sixth Sunday of Easter—*White*
Ascension Day (sixth Thursday of Easter)—*White*

---

*The number of Sundays after Christmas, Epiphany, and Pentecost
varies from year to year, but the last Sundays after Epiphany and Pentecost
are always Transfiguration of the Lord and Christ the King respectively.

Seventh Sunday of Easter (may be observed as Ascension Sunday)—*White*

The Day of Pentecost (Eighth Sunday of Easter)—*Red*

SEASON AFTER PENTECOST—from the day after Pentecost through the day before Advent

First Sunday after Pentecost, or Trinity Sunday—*White*

*Second through next-to-last Sunday after Pentecost—*Green*

All Saints' Day—November 1—or All Saints' Sunday—first Sunday in November—*White*

Last Sunday after Pentecost, or Christ the King—*White*

The Basic Colors

White (and also gold) are joyous and festive colors, used during the Christmas and Easter Seasons and on high days during the Seasons after Epiphany and Pentecost.

Purple is the color both of penitence and royalty, used during Advent and Lent.

Red is the color of fire, symbolizing the Holy Spirit and used on the Day of Pentecost and at other times when the work of the Holy Spirit is being emphasized. A deep hue of red symbolizes the blood of Christ and is often used during Holy Week, beginning with Passion/Palm Sunday, and also when martyrs are being commemorated. If a color is used at all on Good Friday, deep red is increasingly preferred. Red is also an appropriate color for evangelistic services, for ordinations and consecrations, for anniversaries and homecomings, and for civil observances such as Thanksgiving. Red is an intense color which the church has traditionally used for particular days or for short periods rather than continuously for a whole season.

Green is the color of growth and is used in the Seasons after Epiphany and after Pentecost except when special days call for white or red.

Visual Suggestions for the Days and Seasons

Advent. Purple or blue. An Advent wreath with four candles, which appropriately match the color your church is using on the four Sundays in Advent, strengthens the anticipation. This wreath is traditionally suspended so as to suggest the shape of a tree, and one more candle is lighted on each successive Sunday. Christmas trees may be decorated with Christian symbols known as chrismons, which are described in the *Worship Alive* leaflet *Symbols of His Coming: Four Chrismon Programs,* available from Cokesbury or Discipleship Resources (W098L). The leaflet *Las Posadas,* available from Discipleship Resources (S391L), describes a Hispanic processional celebration. Other Advent symbols include a plumb line (Amos), trumpets, scales of justice, and the root or tree of Jesse.

Christmas Season. White or gold, or the finest and most joyful available. Fine and elegant textures. A creche or manger scene may be used throughout this season, with the Wise Men being added when

Epiphany is celebrated. The Wise Men traditionally represent the races of humanity, which can be suggested by the colors of their faces and hands. Three crowns also symbolize the Wise Men, and in the Hispanic world Epiphany is celebrated as "Three Kings." The gifts of the Wise Men—gold, frankincense (which may be burned as incense), and myrrh—are also appropriate for Epiphany.

Season After Epiphany. Green, except that white is used on the first and last Sundays in honor of the baptism and the transfiguration of the Lord. The baptism of the Lord is an excellent time for baptisms and for renewing our own baptismal covenant, with such symbols of baptism as water, a baptismal shell, a descending dove, and a cross standing in water. Symbols on each Sunday after Epiphany may be derived from the manifestation (epiphany) of Christ described in the lectionary reading from the Gospel, such as the wedding at Cana (one or six water jars) and the Transfiguration (Christ in a blaze of glory, with shining garments).

Lent. Purple, gray, dark earth colors, or any somber hues. Rough coarse textures such as burlap. From Passion/Palm Sunday through Holy Week a deep hue of red may be used to symbolize the blood of Christ. Symbols of the Passion that are appropriate, especially in Holy Week, include crown of thorns, whip, ladder, INRI, sponge, spears, nails, crowing cock, drops of blood, and bag of coins. At the beginning of the Passion/Palm Sunday Service the people may process with palm fronds or green branches of any tree or shrub. Later in the service the long Gospel lesson may be read dramatically. All crosses may be veiled during Lent, especially during Holy Week, and most especially on Good Friday. On Maundy Thursday any of the above colors, or white, may be used; and all visuals may be stripped from the chancel at the end of the service and not replaced until the first service of Easter. The candle-extinguishing service of Tenebrae may be used on either Maundy Thursday or Good Friday. No colors, flowers, or decorative materials should be used on Good Friday except, perhaps, representations of the way of the cross; the chancel should be bare of cloth, candles, or anything else not actually used in the service. The Lord's Supper should not be celebrated between Maundy Thursday and the first service of Easter.

Easter Season. White or gold, or the finest and most joyful available. Fine and elegant textures. If possible, the transformation from Lenten to Easter visuals occurs at the lighting of the Paschal Candle at the first service of Easter. For this service and for the remainder of the Easter Season the Paschal Candle may be used as described on page 53. At the first lighting of the Paschal Candle, the congregation may also light candles and the cross may be unveiled, signifying the resurrection. Bolts of brightly colored cloth may be slit lengthwise and hung across the church, and flowers may be used in profusion. Other symbols for the season include the phoenix, butterflies, peacocks, pomegranate, or (especially for Ascension) abstract images such as a vertical arrow. Flame red to signify the Holy Spirit may be used with white and gold throughout the season and is appropriately the dominant color on the Day of Pentecost. Appropriate symbols for the Day of Pentecost include a descending dove, tongues of flame, symbols of the church (ship, rainbow), and a downward arrow.

Season After Pentecost. Green, except that white is used on the first and last Sundays (Trinity and Christ the King) and on All Saints' Day or Sunday, and red may be used as indicated on pages 67-68. Freedom, variety, and creativity ought to be encouraged during this season. Combinations of colors and colors other than the basic four are appropriate. One possibility is to change with the season from the yellow-green of spring through the bluer green of summer to the red, yellow, and brown tones of autumn. The Scripture lessons each Sunday may suggest ideas by their key images, words, or phrases. On Trinity Sunday symbols of the Trinity such as the equilateral triangle, trefoil, fleur-de-lis, triquetra, and three intertwined circles, are especially appropriate. Symbols of All Saints' include a cloud of witnesses, silhouettes representing all races and both sexes, the names of great Christians in history, and the names of those in the congregation who have died in the past year. For Christ the King any symbol of royalty may be used (crown, orb, or scepter, especially when these contain, or are combined with, a cross); and Christ may be pictured as ruler of all, sitting on a throne and blessing the world.

[PREPARING FOR SERVICES]

All of the previous information is background for your practical week-by-week responsibilities. It is important that you and those who work with you list specific weekly and seasonal duties and also specific things that you are to do each time there is Holy Communion, Holy Baptism, a wedding, a funeral or memorial service. These responsibilities should be agreed upon under the leadership of your pastor and in consultation with any other persons or organizations in your congregation who relate to these responsibilities. It is important that *someone* be clearly assigned to a particular responsibility. What you decide should be put into writing, distributed to all persons involved, and kept where it can easily be referred to, so that everyone is clear about his or her responsibilities. Your church procedures should be tailored to fit your local situation, but the guidelines which follow are general suggestions which you can adapt and build upon.

General Responsibilities

1. Keep in close touch with your pastor and make sure you know when every service is to be held

and when there will be any special needs or any
occasions such as baptisms, Communion, weddings, or funerals for which you will have
responsibilities.
2. Work in cooperation with the custodian to be
sure the chancel is kept clean. Regularly wipe,
and when necessary polish, the Lord's table,
pulpit, baptismal font, rail, and other chancel
furnishings.
3. Set up a regular schedule and procedure for
checking, cleaning, and polishing all the items
entrusted to your care.
4. Check ahead to make sure that the seasonal
paraments and other items that you will need in
the near future are ready for use. Avoid the crisis
of discovering a day or two before it is needed an
article that needs to be cleaned or repaired.
5. If you have a rotating weekly, monthly, or
seasonal schedule of assignments, make sure
that persons are reminded in advance when it is
their turn.

Before and After Every Service

1. Check to determine the correct color for the
paraments, change them when indicated, and
properly store those that are removed from the
chancel.
2. Be sure that all linens, paraments, altarware, and
other appointments and decorations are spotless
and in perfect repair.
3. Check all candles to see that they are ready for
use. Clean, trim, and replace them as needed.

4. Be sure that everything needed for the service—such as candle lighters, offering plates, and seasonal appointments—is in its proper place.
5. See that flowers are properly placed, arranged, and (if necessary) watered. See that flower donations are properly acknowledged in the bulletin or by other appropriate ways.
6. Even though all these preparations have been made during the preceding week, come early enough before the service to check and be prepared to correct anything that is unexpectedly amiss.
7. After the service dispose of the flowers in whatever way that has been agreed upon or is indicated by their condition. If they are to be taken to a hospital or home, make sure that they have been taken or that there is a plan for delivering them. Be sure that no empty vases or containers or wilted flowers are left in the chancel during the week.

Holy Communion

1. Be sure that you are growing in your own understanding of Holy Communion—by participation in the Sacrament whenever possible, by discussing it with your pastor, and by reading resources such as those listed in the bibliography.
2. Be sure that you know from regular consultation with your pastor when Holy Communion is to be celebrated and exactly what is expected of you, including how you are to prepare the bread and

wine, how it is to be served, and what, if any, new Communion ware will be needed in the near future.

3. Prepare the Communion bread and wine and care for the Communion ware with the reverence that is appropriate to their holy nature and purpose. Develop whatever skills you can in order to carry out this ministry more effectively.

4. Bread should, if possible, be homemade especially for Communion. You should be aware that there is a growing trend to return to the New Testament and early Christian practice of using a common loaf of real bread instead of wafers, pellets, or cubes of shortbread. Read *The Bread That We Bake* (listed in the bibliography), gather other bread recipes as you have opportunity, and choose under the direction of your pastor which one is best for your church. If someone else is to bake the bread, be sure that this person understands exactly what is expected and is given ample notice.

5. According to the rubrics in *The Book of Hymns* and *The Book of Worship*, "the pure, unfermented juice of the grape shall be used" as the Communion wine. This means that no juice other than that of the grape and no artificial grape-flavored drink are acceptable. Ideally this, like the bread, should be homemade. Perhaps someone in your congregation grows grapes and could make this possible in your Communion services.

6. The same rubrics also state regarding the Lord's table that "the elements of bread and wine shall be placed thereon," and that "it is our custom to

deliver the elements into the hands of the people." So-called self-service Communion, where the bread and wine are set out in advance on the rail rather than on the Lord's table, and where persons serve themselves, does serious violence to the symbolism of Holy Communion, in which Christians serve *others* rather than themselves.

7. The Communion bread is traditionally placed on a special plate called a paten, reserved for that purpose. The Communion wine is traditionally placed in a fine metal flagon or a glass cruet, reserved for that purpose, from which at the proper time in the service the wine is poured into a special cup called a chalice, reserved for that purpose. Chalices and patens have traditionally been made of silver or gold, but ceramic and other materials are often used today.

Chalice

Paten

Flagon

Cruet

With the increased use of whole loaves of bread today, patens are often larger than formerly, and sometimes the bread is brought to the table in a bread basket. Small individual cups are often used instead of a common cup for the wine. When a common cup is used, persons often dip their bread into the cup rather than drink from it. When bread is to be dipped into the cup some ministers prefer to have a spoon handy for removing particles of it from the wine in the cup. Special spoons with a perforated bowl are made for this purpose, but any fine spoon may be used.

8. If individual cups are used, equipment for filling them and cleaning them efficiently is available from Cokesbury and other church supply houses.

9. Check with the pastor during the week before the Communion Service to verify details, such as the approximate number of persons to prepare for and the best time to set the Lord's table for Communion. If there is to be a Saturday wedding or funeral in the church, for instance, wait until after it is over to set the table. Be sure the church will be open and that the custodian knows that you will be there.

10. Be sure, well in advance, that the Communion linens are ready for use.

11. The paraments should reflect the day or season of the Christian year and should be white only if that is what the day or season calls for. There has been much confusion over this question because many persons have confused the paraments with the white linens.

12. There will be other details in the preparation which vary with the customs of congregation and the preferences of the pastor, which you will need to incorporate into your local guidelines under the direction of your pastor.

13. After the service is over, the Communion ware and Communion linens should immediately be removed from the chancel for cleaning.
14. Follow your pastor's directions regarding the disposition of any remaining bread and wine such as taking them to the sick and shut-in, reverently consuming them, or reverently pouring on or into the ground.

Holy Baptism

1. Be sure that you are growing in your own understanding of Holy Baptism—by your participation as a member of the congregation whenever the Sacrament is celebrated, by discussing it with your pastor, and by reading resources such as those listed in the bibliography.
2. Be sure that you know from regular consultation with your pastor when Holy Baptism is to be celebrated and exactly what is expected of you.
3. Water is the element used for the celebration of Holy Baptism. It has a rich variety of powerful symbolic meanings, which the books listed in the bibliography describe. According to the rubrics in *The Book of Hymns* and *The Book of Worship*, "This Sacrament may be administered by sprinkling, pouring, or immersion." That is, the water may be sprinkled or poured over the person's head, or the person may be totally immersed in the water—as the person, or the person's parents, may choose.

4. The same rubrics state, "This Sacrament should be administered in the church in the presence of the people in a stated hour of worship."

5. This is done at the baptismal font, which was mentioned on page 15. The font should stand on the floor and be large enough to symbolize the importance of baptism in our faith; that is, it should be in balance with the pulpit and the Lord's table. It should contain a bowl large enough not only to hold the water but also to catch it when it is sprinkled or poured. Fonts may be made in a variety of materials and in many shapes. Many have covers. Since it is not customary to vest the font with paraments, the font itself should be as attractive as possible and may be decorated with symbols. Some ministers use a shell to pour from; others use their hands.

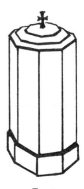

Font

Being used increasingly today is the ancient practice in which the water is carried to the font in a pitcher (traditionally called a ewer) and

79

ceremonially poured into the font, after which the minister gives thanks over the water for all that God has done as symbolized in baptism.

6. Some United Methodist churches have a pool called a baptistry in which they immerse persons who request this mode of baptism; others make arrangements as needed to hold such baptisms in a nearby church that has a baptistry or in an outdoor body of water.

7. Be sure that the font and the bowl—also the ewer and shell, if you have them—are kept clean and polished.

8. Prior to any service at which baptism is to be celebrated, water should be placed either in the ewer or in the bowl of the font. Check to be sure whether your minister prefers the water to be warmed, at room temperature, or cool. It is desirable to have a towel placed at the font, to dry the person who has just been baptized. If a shell is used for pouring, it is laid on top of the towel.

9. If your church uses a Paschal Candle (see pages 53-54) it should be placed near the font except during the Easter Season and lighted whenever there is a baptism. White candles may be lit from the Paschal Candle and presented to the baptized persons, who in turn may wish to light theirs each year on the anniversary of their baptism.

10. When baptism by immersion is requested, special clothing is normally used by both minister and candidates. Someone familiar with baptizing by immersion can usually be found to

loan such clothing, assist in preparations, and coach the minister and others who are to participate. If this occurs often in your church, your minister will probably develop the necessary skills and procure the needed clothing.

Weddings

1. Though many weddings are not held in churches, those that are concern the Altar Guild. Church weddings are becoming, and rightly so, regarded as services of worship focused on God, rather than ceremonies focused on people. This should be reflected in the environment of worship. Flowers, candles, and other decorations should not be arranged so as to obscure or overshadow the cross, the Lord's table, the pulpit, or the baptismal font; and they should not interfere with the appropriate movement of the minister or any other participant.
2. Some prefer that paraments and stoles for weddings be in the liturgical color of the day or season, while others prefer to use white for weddings. Find out what your pastor wishes to use and see that the paraments and stoles are in place before the wedding.
3. Some churches use a kneeling cushion or prie-dieu on which the couple kneel for prayer. This must be cleaned and stored when not in use and then properly placed before the service in accordance with the wishes of your pastor.

4. If additional candles and candelabra are used, it should be only with the approval and under the direction of the pastor.

5. A Service of Christian Marriage may be a full service of the Word and Holy Communion. Whether this is appropriate in a given situation is for the pastor and the couple to decide, and if this is to be done the pastor should give those who prepare for Communion ample advance notice and let them know exactly what is expected of them. The whole congregation should be invited to receive Communion, although not everyone may choose to do so; and you should make appropriate Communion preparations at the direction of your pastor.

6. It is important that the chancel be put back in order for the next service. Since weddings are frequently on Saturday, it is often necessary to schedule this work carefully. Flowers left from the wedding should be used again only if they are still fresh.

Funerals and Memorial Services

1. Funerals and memorial services, like weddings, are often not held in churches; but when they are, the Altar Guild has certain important responsibilities. Church funerals and memorial services are services of worship focused on God and upon the message of the Christian gospel, and this should be reflected in the environment of worship. Flowers, candles, and other decorations should not overshadow the cross. Neither

they nor the coffin should obscure the Lord's table, pulpit, or baptismal font, nor interfere with the appropriate movement of the minister or any other participant. The coffin should remain closed.

2. Preferences vary as to the appropriate color for paraments and stoles at funerals and memorial services. White or green are increasingly preferred, but purple and black are still sometimes used. Others prefer to use the liturgical color of the day or season. Find out what your pastor wishes to use and see that they are in place before people arrive.

3. There is much to be said for covering the coffin completely with a special cloth called a pall while it is in the church. A pall can be purchased from a church supply house, but many congregations prefer to make their own pall. The same pall is used in a congregation for all funerals; and thus all coffins, however plain or extravagant, are vested as equals before the table of the Lord. The predominant color in most palls today is white, usually with a large cross design in some other color such as purple, gold, or green. The pall is placed over the coffin before it is brought into the place of worship and is removed in the narthex after the service. Flowers are never placed on top of the pall. It is important that the pall be clean and free of wrinkles for each funeral. The pall may be laid over the last pew in readiness for the arrival of the coffin.

4. In many funerals today the traditional custom of carrying the coffin in procession from the

narthex to the front of the nave has been restored. The traditional processional order is: processional cross, Paschal Candle and/or processional candles, presiding minister, assisting minister(s), and the coffin carried by pallbearers. Prior to such a procession, the processional cross, Paschal Candle, and/or processional candles should be in readiness in the narthex. The Paschal Candle holder should be in place near where the head of the coffin will be, the processional candle holders near the place where the head and the foot of the coffin will be, and the processional cross holder in its usual place in the chancel.

5. The coffin is placed, or brought by procession, to the front of the nave in the center aisle at right angles to the Lord's table. The head is closest to the congregation unless the person was ordained, in which case the head may be toward the Lord's table. The Paschal Candle is placed in its holder at the head, the processional candles are placed at the head and foot, and the processional cross is placed in its usual place in the chancel.

6. A funeral or memorial service is itself usually a service of the Word, and it may be a full service of Word and Holy Communion. The pastor and the bereaved family decide whether or not this is appropriate in a given situation. If it is, those who prepare for Communion should be given as much notice as possible and told exactly what is expected of them. Not everyone in the congregation may choose to receive Communion, and

no one should feel under pressure to do so, but all should be invited.

7. After the service it is important that the pall be carefully stored, the processional cross and candles placed in readiness for the next service, and the Paschal Candle returned to its proper place in the chancel (see page 53).

[FOR FURTHER READING]

As you work, you will have questions that are not answered in this book. You will want to keep growing in your understanding and skills. Here are some suggestions for your further reading and reference.

Specifically for Altar Guilds

The *Altar Guild Calendar*, to be published by Abingdon Press each year beginning in 1985, is a companion piece to this book. It enables the Altar Guild to follow the days and seasons of the Christian year, with suggested flower arrangements.

Two excellent Altar Guild manuals from other denominations are: Stauffer, S. Anita. *The Altar Guild: A Guide for the Ministry of Liturgical Preparations*. Philadelphia: Fortress Press, 1978, (Lutheran). Gent, Barbara, and Betty Sturges. *The Altar Guild Book*. Wilton, Conn.: Morehouse-Barlow Co., 1982, (Episcopal). While they reflect denominational practices that often differ from those of United Methodists, they contain much valuable information and are useful references.

Altar Guild Manual for First Centenary United Methodist Church (available from the church, 419 McCallie Avenue, Chattanooga, Tenn. 37402) is an excellent description of how one outstanding local church Altar Guild functions.

Inman, Jack. *Floral Art in the Church*. Nashville: Abingdon Press, 1968. Out of print but still available in many church libraries.

Raynor, Louise, and Kerr, Carolyn. *Church Needlepoint.* Wilton, Conn.: Morehouse-Barlow Co., 1976.

The *Worship Alive* series (Discipleship Resources, P.O. Box 189, Nashville, Tenn. 37202) includes the following booklets of particular interest to Altar Guilds:

Eslinger, Richard. *The Bread That We Bake.* (W088L). Communion bread recipes and suggestions.

Gannaway, Marian. *Symbols of His Coming: Four Chrismon Programs.* (W098L).

Hickman, Hoyt L. *What Color This Sunday? An Introduction to the Christian Year.* (W105L).

Kriewald, Diedra. *Vesting the House of the Lord.* (W108L).

Riddle, Florence. *Acolyte Training.* (W079L).

General Books on Worship

Davies, J. G., ed. *The Westminster Dictionary of Worship.* Philadelphia: The Westminster Press, 1979. A comprehensive reference book.

Hickman, Hoyt L. *How We Worship.* Forthcoming in 1984 from Abingdon Press. Provides a basic understanding of worship and is a companion piece to this book.

White, James F. *Introduction to Christian Worship.* Nashville: Abingdon Press, 1980. A more advanced book.

Whittemore, Carroll E., ed. *Symbols of the Church.* Nashville: Abingdon Press, 1959.

Willimon, William H. *Remember Who You Are.* Nashville: The Upper Room, 1980. A simple United Methodist explanation of Holy Baptism.

―――. *Sunday Dinner.* Nashville: The Upper Room, 1981. A simple United Methodist explanation of Holy Communion.

Supplemental Worship Resources Series

These books, published by Abingdon Press, provide basic understandings of United Methodist worship services.

A Service of Baptism, Confirmation, and Renewal (SWR 2), 1980.

Word and Table: A Basic Pattern of Sunday Worship for United Methodists (SWR 3), 1980. Sunday worship with and without Holy Communion.

A Service of Christian Marriage (SWR 5), 1979.

Seasons of the Gospel: Resources for the Christian Year (SWR 6), 1979. Includes a history and interpretation of the Christian year and suggestions for each day and season.

A Service of Death and Resurrection (SWR 7), 1979. An introduction to funerals and memorial services, with resources.

From Ashes to Fire: Services of Worship for the Seasons of Lent and Easter (SWR 8), 1979.

From Hope to Joy, Services of Worship and Additional Resources for the Seasons of Advent and Christmas (SWR 15), 1984.

[Glossary and Index]

ACOLYTE / 56
A server or lay assistant, usually a youth or child, one of whose functions is to light and extinguish candles.

ADVENT / 65, 67, 68
The first season in the Christian year.

ALB / 47
A traditional white worship vestment.

ALL SAINTS' DAY / 67, 71
November 1. May be celebrated as All Saints' Sunday on the first Sunday in November.

ALTAR / 14-19
The Lord's table, holy table, Communion table, altar table, where the feast of the Lord's Supper is held.

ALTAR GUILD / 9-11
A committee devoted to the care of the altar table and its surroundings.

ALTAR RAIL / 15
A railing enclosing the chancel at which persons kneel to pray, to commit themselves to Christ, and to receive Holy Communion.

ANTEPENDIUM / 40-43
A hanging for the front of the pulpit or lectern.

ASCENSION DAY / 66
The fortieth day after Easter.

ASH WEDNESDAY / 66
The seventh Wednesday before Easter.

BAPTISM OF THE LORD / 66
The first Sunday after Epiphany.

BAPTISTRY / 80
The place in the church where the baptismal font is located, or a large pool in the church for baptism by immersion.

CERECLOTH / 36
The bottom linen on the Lord's table.

GLOSSARY AND INDEX

CHALICE / 38, 76
The large cup used at Holy Communion.

CHANCEL / 14-21
The focal area in a room designed for worship, in which the Lord's table and pulpit are located.

CHRISMON / 68
From the words "Christ monograms." Symbols of Christ used to decorate Christmas trees.

CHRIST CANDLE / 53, 70
The white candle in the center of the Advent wreath, which is lighted on Christmas.

CHRIST THE KING / 66, 71
The Last Sunday of the Christian year.

CHRISTIAN YEAR / 64-71
The year as arranged by the church for celebrating the life and work of Christ.

CHRISTMAS DAY / 65
December 25, the celebration of Christ's birth.

CHRISTMAS EVE / 65
Begins at sunset December 24 and is part of Christmas, since the days of the Christian year traditionally begin at sunset the previous day.

CHRISTMAS SEASON / 65-66, 68-69
From sunset December 24 through January 6. The sea-

son celebrating the birth and manifestation (epiphany) of Christ.

CHURCH YEAR / 64-71
The Christian year.

CINCTURE / 48
The rope belt worn with an alb.

COMMUNION TABLE / 14-21
The Lord's table, holy table, altar table, where the feast of the Lord's Supper is held.

CRUET / 76
A glass vessel in which wine and water for Holy Communion is brought to the Lord's table.

DOSSAL / 20
A fabric hanging behind and above the Lord's table.

EASTER DAY / 66, 70-71
The Sunday after the first full moon on or after the first day of spring, which can take place as early as March 22 and as late as April 25, on which Christ's resurrection is celebrated.

EASTER EVE / 66, 70-71
Begins at sunset the day before Easter and is part of Easter, since the days of the Christian year traditionally begin at sunset the previous day.

EASTER SEASON / 66, 70-71
"The Great Fifty Days" from sunset Easter Eve through

EASTER SEASON, *continued*
the Day of Pentecost. The climatic season of the Christian year.

EASTER VIGIL / 53, 66, 70-71
The ancient service on Easter Eve, now widely being restored, in which the passage of Christ from death to resurrection is celebrated and during which it is traditional for persons to be baptized and, more recently, the congregation to renew its baptismal covenant.

ELEMENTS / 74-78
The bread and wine used in Holy Communion and the water used in Holy Baptism.

EPIPHANY / 66, 68-89
January 6, the celebration of the epiphany (which means "manifestation") of God in Jesus Christ. It is traditionally associated with the visit of the Wise Men and in Hispanic cultures is also known as Three Kings. It can also be celebrated as Epiphany Sunday on the first Sunday in January.

**EPIPHANY,
SEASON AFTER** / 66, 69
From January 7 through the day before Lent. On the Sundays in this season the Gospel lessons in the lectionary recount various manifestations (epiphanies) of God in Jesus Christ.

EUCHARIST / 74-78
A term for the service of the Lord's Supper or Holy Communion, derived from the Greek word for thanksgiving.

EWER / 79-80
The pitcher in which water for baptism is carried to the font.

FAIR LINEN / 36-40, 77-78
The top white linen cloth covering the top (mensa) of the Lord's table.

FALL / 40-43
A hanging for the front of the Lord's table, pulpit, or lectern.

FLAGON / 76
A covered pitcher-like vessel in which wine for Holy Communion is brought to the Lord's table.

FONT / 15-16, 79-80
A term, derived from the Latin word for fountain, for the receptacle of stone, metal, or wood which holds the water for Holy Baptism.

FRONTAL / 41
A hanging that covers the entire front of the Lord's table.

FRONTLETS / 42
Narrow strips that hang from the front of the Lord's table, or from the front and back, part way to the floor. Also known as altar antependia.

GOOD FRIDAY / 66, 67, 70
A term probably derived from "God's Friday." The Friday before Easter, on which Christ's crucifixion and death are commemorated.

GRADINE / 20, 52, 54, 58
A term derived from the Latin word for step. A step or shelf at the rear of the Lord's table, also known as the retable.

HOLY WEEK / 66, 69-70
The week beginning with Passion/Palm Sunday and preceding Easter.

INTINCTION / 38, 76-77
A term derived from the Latin word for dip. The practice of dipping the bread into the wine as it is served at Holy Communion.

LECTERN / 15, 16, 40-43
A reading stand sometimes placed in the chancel in addition to the pulpit.

LECTIONARY / 64-65
A schedule of recommended Scripture lessons for the days of the Christian year. The Common (or Ecumenical) Lectionary used by many denominations throughout the world today is based on a three-year cycle.

LENT / 66, 69-70
The preparatory season before Easter, from Ash Wednesday until sunset Easter Eve.

LINENS / 35-40, 73, 78
The white linen cloths used on the top (mensa) of the Lord's table, with the Communion bread and wine, and as baptismal towels.

LITURGY
A term derived from the Greek word for public service. The ordered corporate worship of the church.

MAUNDY (Holy)
THURSDAY / 66, 70
The Thursday before Easter. The term "Maundy" is derived from the Latin word for commandment (John 13).

MENSA / 36
A term for the top of the Lord's table, derived from the Latin word for table.

MISSAL STAND or
MISSAL PILLOW / 59
A stand or pillow on the Lord's table which holds the service book at a suitable angle and distance for easy reading by the minister.

NARTHEX / 13, 83-84
The entrance hall of a church building.

NAVE / 13-14, 83-84
A term for the area where the congregation worships, derived from the Latin word for ship.

PALL / 83, 85
A large cloth placed over the coffin.

PARAMENTS / 35, 40-44, 65-71, 73, 77, 81, 83
Colored cloth hangings used on the Lord's table, pulpit, or lectern.

PASCHAL CANDLE / 53, 70, 80, 84, 85
The large candle placed near the Lord's table and lighted during the Easter season, placed near the font at other seasons and lighted for Holy Baptism, and placed lighted near the head of the coffin at church funerals.

PASSION/PALM SUNDAY / 66, 69-70
The beginning of Holy Week. Passion Sunday and Palm Sunday were formerly successive Sundays but are now celebrated together on the Sunday before Easter.

PATEN / 76
A plate for the bread used at Holy Communion.

PENTECOST, DAY OF / 67, 70-71
The Sunday seven weeks after Easter when the coming of the Holy Spirit upon the disciples is celebrated. The term is derived from the Greek for fiftieth day.

PENTECOST, SEASON AFTER / 67, 71
The half of the Christian year from the day after Pentecost through the day before Advent. It is *not* the Pentecost season; that term, when used, is another way of designating the great fifty days of the Easter season.

PRIE-DIEU / 81
A French term, meaning pray God, for a prayer desk at which couples sometimes kneel at weddings.

PROCESSIONAL CROSS / 52-53
A cross on a tall pole used to lead processions.

PROCESSIONAL TORCH or PROCESSIONAL CANDLE / 56
A large candle on a tall pole carried in processions.

PULPIT / 15-17, 40-43
The raised reading desk in the chancel from which the Scriptures are read and preached.

PURIFICATOR / 38
A square linen napkin used to wipe the rim of the chalice during the serving of Holy Communion.

REREDOS / 20
A carved stone or wood panel behind and above the Lord's table.

GLOSSARY AND INDEX

RETABLE / 20, 52, 54, 55, 59
A step or shelf at the rear of the Lord's table, also known as a gradine.

SANCTUARY / 12
In traditional usage, the immediate area around the Lord's table. In common usage, the whole room designated for worship.

SANCTUARY LAMP / 56
A candle suspended from the ceiling or mounted on the wall near the Lord's table and constantly burning throughout the week, also referred to as an "eternal light." In Roman Catholic usage it signifies the presence of Christ in the reserved sacrament; in Protestant usage it signifies Christ's presence in the church.

STOLE / 46, 48-50, 65, 81, 83
A long colored cloth band worn around the neck and falling from the shoulders of ordained elders and over the left shoulder of deacons.

SUPERFRONTAL / 41
A parament which extends the length of the front of the Lord's table but hangs down only six to twelve inches.

TRANSEPTS / 13-14
Seating areas at right angles to the nave, forming the arms of a cross-shaped church.

TRANSFIGURATION OF THE LORD / 66, 69
The last Sunday in the season after Epiphany.

TRINITY SUNDAY / 67, 71
The first Sunday after Pentecost.

VEIL / 36-37, 44
A cloth sometimes placed over the bread and cup before and after Holy Communion, or over a cross or other joyous picture or symbol on Good Friday, or during Holy Week, or throughout Lent.

VESTMENTS / 46-50
The distinctive clothing (albs, stoles, robes, and such) worn by those taking leadership roles in public worship.